Me and God Locked in a Room and Only One of Us has the Key

lynn w. francis

Contents

Take this:

My wholeness
My half-empty

My undying love
My long lost eternity

It's all I have to give

Before

In all that was before this,
I knew you then.
I loved you.

The Tree Still Standing After the Storm

Even when

all my havoc has cried

And the dogs of war have slipped me by

Still you stay, unmoved remain

You know my heart, you say my name

What
and
who
and
how
are
you?

Unbid, yet through my heart you go

Tread the paths only I have known

You must be magic, must be real

To know both who I am and why I feel

"Don't Mind Me, I'm the Worst of Us"

Where are we tonight
Is this heaven or hell
Or is purgatory really just an all-night diner
On an infinite night
Serving our glutton hearts the comfort of familiar evils
And sexual immorality with a side of ketchup
(Ketchup goes with anything)

We are good people
I have no doubt
Ready to die for our faith
But elbow deep in blasphemy
Do we live for it?
(I rearrange the sugar packets)

What right do I have to notice these failings anyway
I have entire trees growing out of my own eyes
My sins are a forest so thick that if I fell
I wouldn't make a sound
I've already betrayed my doctor, myself, my priest
And all has been forgiven
(What's another plate on the tab?)

Mantra

I have not lost anything.

Things don't just stop existing

Discarded shopping lists go on to paper shopping carts and then parking lots
Butterflies crawl backward into chrysalis and their wings dissolve
And I'll call that the miracle of life
As I've been taught to do
Things don't just stop existing
They go on

No, they aren't lost.

Your family didn't stop existing

I didn't stop existing, though the rearview mirror doesn't recognize me
Damn it, I kept walking as my ponytail evolved into a buzzcut, grew into a
tangle around my hands
Bedroom carpet slowly wore down to the floorboards from pacing
Back and forth, how to forgive
How to hold my heart back
I am not lost

My family isn't lost.

Fathers don't just stop existing

Though they crawl back into chrysalis through an opening too small for
anyone to follow
Dissolving back into whatever they were before they had a responsibility to
uphold
And they call that life
As they've been taught to do
They aren't lost, they just didn't want to be found
And we, well, we went on

Love isn't lost.

It didn't just stop existing

Didn't fly up from the carnival and burst in the sky when I let it go
Nor does it remain the way it once was
It's a wretched thing, dragging itself though night after night
Hoping transformation is found at the top of the cellar stairs, hoping there's more than just surviving
As forgiveness, or a fence
Love goes on

The Things You Can't See in a Snowstorm

People who have frozen to death (if found)
  are quite often found completely naked
This is because when you are cold enough
  your brain stops understanding what you feel
The snow becomes hot coals under the feet
  shivers pour like fresh sweat on the way down
To survive this burning, to cool the heat
  they begin to strip, begin to wander
  away from anyone who could help them
  until the cold— the heat— swallows them up
  and their knees beg for mercy from the snow
Then of course, dark death only comes faster
  hypothermia reaching crescendo
  in a song I too heard, misunderstood
I have known the snow that burns like hellfire
  fingertips like embers losing their grip
  shivers pouring like sweat on the way down
Sure I was burning at the stake when warmth
  was the only thing that could still save me
You were right there and I wouldn't see you
  focused on the proximity of death
You were right there and instead I trusted
  the cold to save me but it killed, it killed

Made Not Mistaken

if I was made
not mistaken
explain
the eyes that never learned
to be anything but rivers
explain
the mind that holds happiness
with the hand grenade
explain
the skin under my fingernails
to the scratches on my thighs
explain
the throat suffocating itself
on the thrashing thing of panic
explain
the head that begs to be clouded
the heart that begs to be bled clear
explain
why anyone loved this thing
that would only hurt them
if I was made
not mistaken
explain
why I was made
broken.

A Fear, a Wish:

sometimes   kisses me,
THE MONSTER

and magic comes out

Bitten Tongue

i close my eyes in fear
lost to the plague of despairing
if You are perfect
then You cannot fail me, i can only fail You
and i will, i am
i am always choosing to do so
for this is the only sure thing, that i can fail You
honoring is harder; impossible, unto You
there is nothing of value in my house, so i offer nothing
close the doors, cower in the bathroom
i do not open my eyes, do not speak
brush blood across my forehead
so that perhaps
Your wrath might pass over me
i hold my grieving to my breast
rock back and forth
keep it quiet as i can
afraid that, if heard
i will be given something to cry about

Honesty

Unhinged
They say
Fair enough
As if I am no longer a body
But a door broken down

      No hiding
             The chaos
                  Now

Serpentine

You say
      I am
          free
             but
          free will
      is a rigged
game
      isn't it
          a ploy   But I
              to lure   thrash and
          me into   snap
      the deep   I would rather
woods   bite off
      until   my own foot
          I'm lost   than be
              and   misled
          hunted   by your
      You want me   promises
trapped   of freedom
      wild animal   Look where
          caught   your freedom
              by the paw   has gotten me
          in your   If you made
      snare   the trees
Helpless   then
      so that you   you made
          can be my   the trap
      savior   How
                    could
              I trust
         a hunter
              How
                   could
                      I believe
              a killer
             capable
        of love?

Walking Song

I breathe.

It takes all I have; my lungs are near death tonight

Silk flutters against my chest, whispering over my bare pulse

Grieving, my heart walks against my ribs

Lust and greed hand in hand with fading purity

I know that I exist only because of the hardwood floor that meets my knees, shoulder, cheek

The floor is cold. I breathe.

This life is a blindfold

Without light we heavy sink toward deeds no mortal can undo

No mortal, I say

You, in all your perfect surrender, have made any strength I had pointless

My heart keeps walking. I do not know how to put it down.

Promises wear thin, and obsession isn't something to be toyed with, not in a heart like this one

So I give what I can, though it won't matter, though it isn't nearly enough

Gun to my head, hand to my heart

I refuse to write temptation any more love letters.

Proverb I

What God looks favorably on His children's design to weakness?

Proverb II

O how carefree the life, how fearful the death of the faithless.

Sin/Sinner

Pop quiz:
Who is going to hell?

A) The believer who loves, respects, cherishes, and/or protects a soul whose
body looks the same as their own; might look this way only in certain light
(at odds with precedent order)

B) The believer who hates, condemns, reprimands, excludes, and/or neglects
someone who doesn't conform to the precept of scripture
(and does this in the name of their God)

Today another friend came out as bisexual and
"not a christian"
And I want to ask how they could walk so lightly away from
the realest love I have ever known
But I know too well the fangs kept in the smiling mouths of some
"good Christians"

I have heard, in the last two weeks, three of my Christian friends praise
conversion therapy
And I stand speechless, remembering all the stories I have heard
All the blood left in gay camp sinks, all the darkness and death brought back
To a home that stopped being home after
someone who was supposed to love you
And thought that they did
Sent you to what would soon become the only hell you'd believe in

A post on social media, shared by one of my friends, says
"You cannot hate my sin *and* love the sinner if it's my identity"

A) If this one idea, one want, one part
        Truly is your only definition
        When and how did your other selves evaporate?

B) If there were any other misaligning between
        Where you and I saw the truth
        Wouldn't I still mean as much to you?

C) If I have broken every promise I have ever made
	My lips at once contract and confessional
	Couldn't any other liar know holy Love as well as I?

D) If every kiss I thought a prayer
	Was deemed a sin by such righteous people
	Wouldn't I raise hell to fight for my passion?

Where is the room for discussion
The option to love and not support
To defend and not condone
To believe something and not hurt others to make them believe it too
		(Even if I want you to believe it too
		Either way I do not want you to be unloved
	Either way, you are not unloved)
I do not know what to do
I do not own a steamer trunk, have no way to carry my faith and my doubt
My belief and uncertainty
I do not have enough arms to link with everyone I want to stand up next to

I do not know how to be honest to any of you.

The oft received advice reads shallow,
Ready for printing on pillows and greeting cards:
"Hate the sin, love the sinner"
Harder than it sounds
Not to bear the shield
Not to wield the switch
Because it's hard to know
Where the line is
And which tool is which.

Pop Quiz:
Who does Christ love?

A) Some

B) All

Pews

uniform rows unbroken by

the crowds carrying their pyres

to feed on God at best or

at worst their own desires

Eve and Mistress Grey

You are a wink of smoke from across the table
Tilting a fine china cup back and forth
Offering the future's dark and drowning dregs
If only I drink, if only I trust your fading smile

I beg the tea to swallow me instead

Lamentation

the pavement screams rubber.
      the traffic lights are all green
      I am driving, going south;
o lord;
I have tried to kill the demons
      but my stomach is their mouth

I cried out and trouble answered.
      lord,
      I called for you;
      silence is too thin to hold my grief.
all I knew to give I gave,
      yet the raging dogs of war
      have me in their teeth.

how long will you let me drown
in this draining bottle?
      lord,
      I took the wine for water.
how long?
      will the father ever run out to meet
      the wayward sinning daughter?

o lord,
must I go on fighting alone?
      I cannot hold back the cold;
      your absence is tribulation
I am so weary of the static.
      o lord,
      kill me or kill this contemplation.

Coping Mechanism

Write it down
        down
                down, you're not unholy
                Write a line, she told me
                Put it down in your little black book
                Write a line, not a hook

Take it out
        out
                out, tear free that page
                Take a line, hang the rage
                Ink can be blood if you use it right
                Take a line, tie it tight

Confrontation

WHAT AM I SUPPOSED TO DO?

I am screaming
screaming, screaming, screaming
There is only one place I can go
that can batten me to my body
My fear is gasoline
my anger the key in the ignition
I drive and I make it somehow
another miracle no one died
The chapel door collapses
kindling to my wrath
My fingers dip into cool holiness
baptism burns my eyes
I scream again

(I am here.
I am with you.)

WHAT DO YOU WANT FROM ME?

You.

Startled into a sudden relative-stillness
I shake in my shoes
I am either fear or anger
or both

What?

The room waits for a response
as smoke obscures everything outside
My knees beg for the reverence of the floor
the stained-glass windows beg to be broken
But I only do the unthinkable
I listen

You.

There again but not a voice
not a thought
Just as loud this time
just as quiet
I am not quiet
I am angry

                                        WHAT AM I SUPPOSED TO DO?

                                        Wait.

I understand that, ridiculously
this is meant to be enough
And ridiculously
it is.

Oneirophobia

"I think I know what dying feels like."
The words
choke
through my mouth like
So many string lights being pulled out of my throat
in the safety of our apartment
"What
You don't ask how I know
what I think I know
does it feel like?"

I dreamed it in a dream
As I always do, even when I'm awake
Pavement bites as it catches my fall, again
Gape-mouthed at the burning shock
Fear teaching horror new words for pain
Realization sinking in with the bullet
I am not making it home, will not get another chance
At anything
I have said the last terrible thing I will ever say
My lungs will never again capture the sky
And if you were to hold me after this I will not be here to feel it

I can't remember the last time I held you
In trying to do so I forget to pay attention
I miss the last time I could have looked at you
I miss our last moments together
And I am gone.

The death dreams only started once I wanted to live
the irony of this is not lost on me, nor is the fact
that since finding my own fragile attempt at love I have
a lot more to lose—
so much more to lose than I ever had before

"You will not,
          You pour out the words
          almost desperately
you will not die alone.
I will be there.
I will be with you.
I know
          How could you know?
that God brought us
this far for a reason.
He isn't done with us yet."

          Every muscle strains as I try to believe you
          try so hard that for once I see through myself to heaven
          and believe it too
          Because we know each other the way we do, meaning
          you can look into my soul and
          my soul would know if you were lying to either of us

          So I listen
          trust with all I have this hope-truth of yours
          I attempt to impress your words into myself by
          pounding against my chest as hard as I can
          which is not very hard
          You catch my fist, hold it instead to your heart
          I feel it beating like I want mine to beat
          like I want to keep living
          as long as you do, at least

          Because I do,
"I want to live."
          but for all the times I've been told that's beautiful
          and all the times as I've believed it
          it's no easier to fall asleep

Things Given Up

My rebel cause has died
I think I killed it last night

Now all I want
Is the war to be fought

The struggle ended
Amnesty declared

Wash the flag in my chest white, Lord
I want to surrender to you

Reprise

I know you want to show that you care after this time apart
But a truthful answer to your questions may turn out to be
Your night-black feline crossing the road and my foot flooring the gas
Because my honesty has been known to kill curious cats

I have carved my lonely name into the fragile skin below my collarbone
Just to remind my mirror-image who the real me is
Not some backwards-letter bloodstain holding shut the bathroom door
No, I am the evidence of a heart gilded with butterknife scars

People I know have called these habits darkness and demons
A fact I know too well to be true in my ongoing self-possession
Action, thought, feeling no longer of my own origination
My internal answering machine reminding me that I'm long overdue for an
exorcism

But rereading directions carefully can still leave room for interpretation
Even for something so worthwhile and precarious as baking bread
Please don't mock me as I pull the book from the garbage can a third time
To gently knead scripture into the heart of my vocabulary

Phosphorus: From Phōs (Light) + -phoros (-bringing)

Even if all these internally directed harpoons prove aimed true

The ground opening up earlier than sensibility anticipates

World as I know it drawing to a final close around my aorta

Even in that inescapable curtainfall of a suddenly empty theatre

I will not beg for reprisal nor third chances at rightly done

It is glory enough to have lived the here and now

To have known the enchantment of phosphorus peace

Witnessed the hammer of the sun against the anvil of your eyes

It is enough to know there was a destiny inscribed with my name

To have found again the narrow way in time to slip through

To eternity, despite harpoons

Psalm

in the levity of daylight, in the honesty of night,
o LORD, I will praise you!
        you have loved me when I wanted for nothing,
        not even you.
in my affliction praise turned to curses,
        and in moments I could taste my own tongue
        why do you love me, LORD?
        I only remind myself of blood.

praise be to the LORD of his people!
my faith faltered on the highway,
        my soul wept and I shook with fear,
        uncertain of the way.
be still, anxious heart!
the rearview mirror praises the LORD;
        to see now he laid the road as I went
        to understand he was with me all the while.
he is with me even now!
what joy!
        the assurance that life is not the product of
        chance and madness;
I sing joy to you, o LORD;
        for even in this fallen world
        I was made with intention and love.

LORD, your faithfulness is like the springtime:
for you put your hand among the wreckage
        and the world turned kaleidoscope,
        every broken thing blooming back whole.
o LORD your mystery captivates me,
        your majesty is worthy of praise!
bewilderment and awe are my blessings;
        that you could look at me
        and see more than what I was.

Admission

best laid plans of men and mice
still go wrong.
still Yours go right.

Walking Closet

There's this idea I keep seeing spooled out

about anger really just being grief with a hat on

about grief just being love dressed up with nowhere to go

Maybe everything we are is love wrapped over and over in itself

the confusion and frustration just costume jewelry and coats

If loneliness is just joy never putting on a favorite perfume

if joy is just love taking off a mask

if everything was untangled in our hearts and laid out end to end

maybe we could finally reach eachother in every way that mattered

Fallacy

it isn't the universe
that called your life out from the dark
the universe doesn't care
half of the stars you've ever wished on are dead
wild animals are born with broken legs

the universe is an unmarked grave

Meanwhile

an order exists in which all
lilies and sparrows
are named, are known
are noticed

The Evidence of Worth

You are worth running after
You are worth fighting for
You are worth parting the heavens
And splitting the earth
Cosmos have moved out of love for you
And the proof of this is
You were worth the life
And death
Of a God

Adoration

I look at you

and art pours out.

Love Letters

perhaps all these

perfectly tangled clouds
&
sunlight peeking through them
&
little birds chirping hello from the sidewalk
&
flowering trees perfuming the air
&
precisely timed poetry
&
all the other pretty little accidents of my day

are really someone saying

"here, I saw this and thought of you."

Countdown

Eight Sundays left.
This odd in-between time keeps catching me off guard
Seven.
Then suddenly, four.
These days my knees sink into the mattress
I tuck my necklace under my collar so that you don't choke on silver as we kiss
You break the chain by accident and I forgive you.

Last week, and how was it last week already?
We held a photo of my dying grandfather and hoped he wasn't dying
Prayed that at least you would get the chance to meet him.
You didn't.
I wept for days.
I'm still glad for the praying though
Glad I got a chance to say goodbye even if it was long distance and one-sided.
The earth has a smell to it again.
I don't know when that came back
But it's nice to breathe something good and whole.

Three Sundays left.
Loyal companions fear and doubt still rattle bones
Mine and other people's.
They do not like friend Hope
Moving about in the wind as it does
Lifting my hair from my ear
Brushing a whisper against my cheek.
The uneven time will come to an end awkwardly
Slowly and too quickly and sideways, as it were.
But it comes, it comes.

One Sunday left.
Everything lights up golden and brass in these sun-downs.
I'm glad we were together
even if the time moved strangely.
Chance speaks to my favor
I just might make it.
No Sundays left.
I'm still glad I was here.

History Lesson

i. They say we only know what to call these tiny black eyed pests
With their scritching legs and hungry mandibles
Because once long ago a man named William wrote "grasshopper"
On a blank page
Before then the world lacked the word to say exactly what he meant
And being incontent he created one

ii. Another creator, another time
Somewhere before blank pages existed
But long after they had been thought of
Was also incontent with the lack of world for the word
So he spoke
And it was good

iii. The only reason I know what to call
Everything I become when I see you
Is because
Once upon something before time
Someone said
"Let there be light"

Prophesy

Incorporeal,
death hovers
crosslegged over the grass

withering yellow
in his cool
shadow.

Sighing,
the trees wait
patient for his touch

for the sweet release
of deciduous
sleep.

They know
better than
to call him executioner

to life eternal, death is
but prophecy
of spring.

Cycle

Everything is ending.
Sundowns and ash and dirty dishes and broken hearts all agree on this.
There have always been and will always be goodbyes that haunt you, freshly dug graves, and last drops in a bottle.
This is the way of things: they break. They fail. They give out. Maybe after millennia, maybe after just seconds, and maybe there never could have been enough time for these things to prove themselves but it doesn't matter. Things die.
You begin to understand this as an infant. You're playing your first game of peek-a-boo and suddenly the only face you know vanishes from your sight; you've suffered a great loss. You begin to cry.
You also begin to misunderstand this as an infant. You're playing your first game of peek-a-boo and suddenly a veil falls away; love comes back. You're laughing through the tears.
Things live. Time bends back and forth and warps from a line to a circle and each tiny perfect moment falls just so over the old wounds, and everything you've ever done mattered. This is the way of things: they heal. They grow. They cannot be stopped.
There have always been and there will always be hello nods and smiles between strangers, freshly planted gardens, and first raindrops of spring.
Sunrises and sparks and birthday cakes and first kisses all agree on this.
Everything is beginning.

A Gravedigger, an Empty Tomb

this hallowed ground is heavy with things i haven't said in too long
war torn soil coming up in spades as i exhume something forgotten
revival is a foreign concept to a heart long since buried alive
expectations pile up in their practiced way with preconceived notions of
You and i
until i am six feet down in the dirt and find that for all my digging
this doesn't have to be a grave; life doesn't have to end
for all the complications with which i bind my hands together,
for all the mud in my eyes it is simple after all:
You are alive, so i am alive.

Acknowledgements

Thank you to everyone who made this collection possible. Thank you to the friends who listened to my ravings and read all my rewrites. Thank you to Becky for all the work you've done to help me. Thank you to Hannah for wonderful posing advice and your patience. Thank you to Ellie and Nate for making sure the content and cover of this book made sense. Thank you to Jon; for believing in me so deeply, for your ambitious spirit, for your encouragement, and for your love. This collection wouldn't exist without any of you.
Thank you to all of the people who have encouraged me in my faith and prodded me along the narrow road. Thank you for your prayers.
Lastly, thank you to the one who got me here. This is all for you.
Soli Deo gloria.

www.ingramcontent.com/pod-product-compliance
Lightning Source LLC
Chambersburg PA
CBHW030513130626

46549CB00007B/2971